25 Dec. 69

To my wonderful husband
as we celebrate our
first Christmas together!

Love to you
always,
Trish

A Gallery of California Mission Paintings

A Gallery of California

Mission Paintings
by Edwin Deakin

Edited by Ruth I. Mahood
additional texts by
PAUL MILLS and DONALD C. CUTTER

Produced by the staff of the History Division
Los Angeles County Museum of Natural History

THE WARD RITCHIE PRESS · LOS ANGELES

Foreword

The professional publications of the Los Angeles County Museum of Natural History include two series, *Contributions* and *Bulletins*. In the past, articles, monographs and catalogs in the fields of history and science have appeared under various headings—*Contributions, Science Series, History Leaflet Series* and unnumbered catalogs of exhibitions and collections. To simplify and to standardize matters, all professional publications of the History and Science Divisions of the Museum will now be issued at irregular intervals either as *Contributions*, or as *Bulletins*. The former will contain short, technical papers which may be occasionally gathered in volumes, octavo in size. The latter will contain longer, separate monographs and catalogs, usually quarto in size, although this will depend on the needs of the presentation. Papers in each series are to be numbered consecutively.

These papers are original articles and studies based on the collections and work of the Museum, presenting newly acquired information and understanding in the fields of Anthropology, Botany, Geology, History, Mineralogy, Paleontology, Technology and Zoology.

This publication forms number 3 of the *Bulletin* series in History.

HERBERT FRIEDMANN, *Director*
Los Angeles County Museum of Natural History

First printing November 1966
Second printing November 1967

Copyright © 1966 by The Ward Ritchie Press
Library of Congress Catalog Card Number 66-26519

Lithographed in the United States of America
by Anderson, Ritchie and Simon

Introduction

The History Division is actively engaged in collecting and preserving the documents, manuscripts, graphic arts and realia which will retain for time to come the factual, interesting, and romantic record of California's beginnings and the events which followed: events which made it the "Golden State" of today.

An outstanding part of the Museum's collection of Californiana is the complete set of the twenty-one Franciscan mission paintings by Edwin Deakin. These paintings have been exhibited continuously in the history galleries of the Los Angeles County Museum of Natural History for over thirty years and enjoyed by the thousands of visitors including many school children.

About 1954 it became evident that this collection, which had been on loan, was to be disposed of in the final settlement of his estate. Realizing the historic and documentary importance of these fine representations of the missions, the Museum made plans to purchase them. With the assistance of Howard Willoughby of Piedmont, California, who was interested in the work of Edwin Deakin and has many of his works in his own private collection, the Museum was able to secure this set of paintings for the permanent collection. But it was at this time that the Museum Association (now the Museum Alliance) gave the financial assistance necessary to make possession of them a reality. Thus, as a result of this generosity, the paintings became the permanent property of the Museum in 1959.

Nothing had been done to preserve the paintings during the years of their existence and, although through careful handling they were in good condition, it was decided to give them a thorough cleaning and restoration. This was accomplished and they were attractively mounted and reframed.

Before re-installing them in the California History Gallery, they formed the nucleus of an Edwin Deakin exhibition at the Museum in the fall of 1960. This display also contained other works of art by Mr. Deakin showing him to be a very versatile painter, and also much interested in architectural detail. When the newly refurbished California History Gallery was opened on March 20 1963, the Deakin Mission Paintings became an important part of the exhibit.

Because the accurate portrayal of the architecture and scenic setting of the Franciscan Missions of California by Edwin Deakin preserves such an important part of the early history of California, the History Division decided to present it as Bulletin Number 3 in this series of its publications. It is with the hope that those who read this will more fully appreciate the important and long-lasting results of the work of the padres of the mission period in our history, as well as the painstaking efforts of the artist, Edwin Deakin, to recall the days of California's Missions and El Camino Real.

RUTH I. MAHOOD
Chief Curator of History

STAFF OF THE HISTORY DIVISION

RUTH I. MAHOOD, *Chief Curator of History*
RUSSELL E. BELOUS, *Curator of Western History*
JOHN DEWAR, *Associate Curator of Western-American Art*
WILLIAM MASON, *Associate Curator of Archives*
NORWOOD TEAGUE, *Associate Curator of Industrial Technology*
LILLIAN GOULD, *Secretary*
CAROL ARNOLD, *Preparator*
ELIZABETH NICKS, *Preparator*
JAMES M. ZORDICH, *Preparator*
JAMES BILLIG, *Student Professional Worker*
STEVE BUCHANAN, *Student Professional Worker*
JUDY STURGEON, *Typist-Clerk*
ROBERT WEINSTEIN, *Research Associate in the History of Photography*

Editor for History Bulletin No. 3: RUTH I. MAHOOD
Introduction: RUTH I. MAHOOD
Catalogue and book design: ROBERT WEINSTEIN
Photography: ARMANDO SOLIS
Edwin Deakin text by: PAUL MILLS
*California Missions text by: DR. DONALD C. CUTTER, DR. JOHN E. BAUR

PRINTED BY ANDERSON, RITCHIE AND SIMON, LOS ANGELES

*The Staff of the History Division wishes to express its special appreciation to Father Maynard Geiger, O.F.M. for his assistance in verifying otherwise unobtainable information of mission history.

California's Twenty-one Franciscan Missions

California's twenty-one Franciscan missions, the founding dates of which range from 1769 to 1823, represent a great cultural heritage of the West. As one of the three main institutions of Hispanic colonial control of the frontier, the mission shared honors with the military presidio and the civil pueblo. Far greater in number and much more satisfactorily preserved or reconstructed, the missions provide more tangible evidence of Spanish occupation of old California. Created as large-scale agricultural units calculated to care for the needs of the area's native population, at the inception the missions had coterminous boundaries, where one ceased the next began. Our modern concept of the mission as being a massive, tile-roofed, whitewashed adobe structure consisting of a chapel, an interior patio in the style of southern Spain, and arcaded corridors leading to the priests' quarters and to the storerooms, is at great variance with the original. The modern remains of most missions are merely the heart of a great socio-economic unit. This institution embraced outlying cattle and sheep ranches, workshops and looms, gardens and orchards, Indian villages and irrigation works, substations for occasional worship services away from the main church, and numerous other items.

As institutions the missions had several reasons for existence. Politically, the Spanish crown used these establishments to bring the aborigine into a regular, productive, and tax-paying relationship with government. Socially, the congregating of the Indians made them more amenable to the process of civilization. Religiously, the mission oriented the native to an atmosphere of Catholic Christianity. It was a matter of adding citizens to both the temporal realm of Spain and to the spiritual kingdom of heaven.

Selection of mission sites was largely predetermined for three places in the master plan for occupation of Upper California. Monterey, subsequently moved to nearby Carmel, San Diego, and San Francisco were sites selected before occupation of California began. Exploration of the area soon made known additional sites that were considered appropriate. A fortuitous juxtaposition of such elements as drinking and irrigation water, wood, stone, arable land, and, most important of all, availability of numerous Indians were prerequisites. Generally a site was selected midway between several populous Indian rancherias, or villages. An attempt was made to attract, through gifts or through stimulation of natural curiosity, as many of the local Indians as possible. The Indian was free to come to the mission if he desired. Once there, however, it was not desired that he leave. To the end of maintaining discipline and preventing fugitism among the mission Indian neophytes, a mission guard of soldiers, an *escolta*, was assigned for order and protection. Consisting of four to six men under a corporal, the *escolta* was sufficient for most occasions.

Characteristic of the missions was their coastal orientation, within a very few miles of salt water in the majority of cases. This nearness to the coast and the plan to have the establishments about one day's travel apart resulted in a mission chain approximately 650 miles in length, connected by a trail which became El Camino Real. The geographical area embraced by the missions provided for considerable climatic variation, with great differences in growing season, which coupled with other geographical considerations resulted in some specialization in mission production, such as the fruits of Santa Clara.

The theory of missionization envisioned a brief period of tutelage of perhaps ten years, but the relatively rude local Indians necessitated prolonged extension of time to become civilized. At the end of an appropriate period, mission control was to be withdrawn from the Franciscan fathers and the lands parceled out to the Indians, whereupon spiritual oversight would become the responsibility of the secular clergy with the mission converted into a parish church. The Franciscans, contrary to popular opinion, were at no time owners of the mission establishments under their control, but merely administrators of Indian property during the period of the natives' incompetence. That the situation could not have been otherwise is evident from the vows of poverty of their mendicant order.

The missionaries at each mission, customarily two in number, were forced by the isolation of California and that of their local mission to become jacks-of-all-trades. Traditionally one priest was primarily concerned with the spiritual advance of the mission, while the other tended to temporal affairs. But circumstances forced each to become businessman, farmer, cattleman, trader, explorer, preacher, teacher, manufacturer, physician, builder. The difficult task of teaching the culturally backward Indians was a challenge to the missionary. Indians who had very few technical skills were taught to till the soil, weave blankets, tan hides, manufacture shoes, make soap and pottery and perform myriad other tasks.

For the first several years each mission establishment was most rudimentary. Made of "temporary adobe," brush, rough-hewn timber, and wooden stakes, the early structures were stopgaps. Years later, after much planning, buildings of greater stability were erected. Even these were not always the missions whose likenesses we see today; since for various reasons it became necessary to build again, sometimes occasioned by flood, or earthquake, or the essential lack of suitability of the earlier site.

The role of Father Junípero Serra, founder of the first nine missions and Father President of those establishments, has been well publicized. Father Fermín Francisco de Lasuén, perhaps equally important as successor to Serra, is less well known, though he was founder of an equal number of missions. A third clerical figure of importance, Fray Mariano Payeras, is associated with the golden age of the missions, for he was President when the physical peak was reached.

After the year 1800 plans were laid to extend the mission field in California, and an inland series of establishments was contemplated. After considerable interior exploration by soldiers and missionary fathers, a number of potential sites were found. But Spain's control of California was on the decline, the resources for expansion were not available. Later,

a new sovereign, Mexico, was less interested in missions, and there was great pressure for distribution of land to settlers. Pressure gave way to action and the Franciscan missions were secularized in a process extending over several years during the 1830's. One rationalization for the breakup of the missions was the inherent lack of democracy of these benevolently despotic institutions, a form of control contrary to both the constitutional and economic interests of the Mexican inhabitants. As a result of several decrees the missions were turned over to secular administrators, who cared little for mission preservation: Some land was distributed to the natives, who proved themselves incapable of retaining it: Many Indians were scattered and returned to live with their uncivilized neighbors: Other aborigines became retainers of the various ranchos that were established from the ex-mission lands. The aging Franciscans were relieved of their spiritual oversight. Deterioration of the physical plant of the mission went on gradually, until finally most of the venerable structures were on the point of total loss. Toward the end of the 19th Century local residents took increased interest and gradually since then, the Franciscan chain has been restored or rebuilt. Though not nearly enough of the old buildings have been preserved intact, the combined efforts of church, state and private interests have attempted to re-create Spanish California at its religious zenith. The Catholic church controls most of the old missions, some are schools, some are chapels, most also serve as museums open to the public. The State of California, under its Division of Beaches and Parks, owns several which are essentially museums.

Before the days of commercialized recreation, in a time when California proudly proclaimed its scenic, climatic and historic virtues to the nation, the California missions were a great tourist attraction. As visitors followed the "trail of the green bells" from mission to mission, there was recaptured some of the flavor of a day which refuses to pass into oblivion—the heyday of the Franciscan missions of California.

DONALD C. CUTTER

9

Edwin Deakin - 1838-1923

The art life of the United States since World War II has been marked by the emergence of American artists as international leaders in contemporary art and by the revival of interest in American artists of the past, especially of the nineteenth century. It is still only gradually becoming apparent that, within the particular riches of this country's art, the painters of California between the Gold Rush and World War I deserve to occupy a special and important place.

Edwin Deakin is one of these men. He shared with others of his day a great enthusiasm for landscape painting, but developed a special vein of his own in picturesque, romantic paintings of the California missions and other exotic buildings. Our art image of California in early days could not be the same without him.

He was born in Sheffield, England, May 21, 1838, the son of Robert and Louisa (Williams) Deakin. The Deakins moved to the United States in 1856, and settled in Chicago. Little is known of Deakin's education, either in England or in the United States. To summarize the speculative-sounding statements made by writers about his early years, he appears to have had an adequate education, and to have shown both interest in the arts and talent for it at an early age; he is repeatedly said to have been largely self taught, and he is supposed to have shown an early enthusiasm for ruins and nostalgic, historic architecture. He married Isabel Fox, the daughter of one George Fox of Doncaster, England, in 1865.[1]

His professional career started in Chicago in 1869,[2] which would have put him at 31 years of age. He is supposed to have attracted a considerable patronage there doing portraits of northern Civil War heroes who had been killed in battle, probably based on daguerreotypes, a kind of painting which was popular then both with private individuals and government agencies.[3]

In 1870 Deakin moved to California, at first establishing both his home and his studio in the city of San Francisco.[4] Within a year or so he had established a good reputation for himself as a painter, and there is considerable evidence to show that during the mid 'seventies he was energetically cultivating many aspects of his artistic career.

Deakin figured prominently in the benefit exhibition arranged in November, 1872, by the artists of San Francisco to raise funds for the family of the Mexican artist and San Francisco resident, Fortunato Arriola, who had been lost at sea. All the greats of the day, including William Keith, Albert Bierstadt, Thomas Hill, William Hahn, Samuel Marsden Brookes, G. J. Denny, Erneste Narjot, as well as Deakin, contributed works. Deakin was further honored by having the Mayor of San Francisco, Mayor Alvord, contribute a Deakin painting, *The Sign of the Gate*.[5]

The same year, Deakin was exhibiting with the new San Francisco Art Association, as he did regularly in the following years. He also sketched the countryside around San Francisco and exhibited in the San Francisco Mechanics'

---

[1]*National Cyclopedia of American Biography*, James T. White, New York, 1964.

[2]*The Outlook*, January, 1904, Vol. 76, page 77. Article by Pauline R. Bird, "Painter of California Missions."

[3]Howard Willoughby's letter to Doris Morrison, July 30, 1958.

[4]*National Cyclopedia of American Biography*, op. cit. "Following the Chicago fire of 1871, he settled in San Francisco . . ." however, every other source states 1870, including a book published by Deakin himself, and there are California sketches in the Howard Willoughby collection dated 1870.

[5]*San Francisco Chronicle*, Friday, November 15, 1872, scrapbook transcript. Most of the newspaper references used here are contained in a scrapbook apparently kept by Deakin and now owned by Miss Marjorie Dakin. A transcript of the more informative clippings was made by Mr. Howard Willoughby. The words "scrapbook transcript" following a newspaper reference indicate the information has been taken from this transcript.

Institute fairs.[6] He also joined the new Bohemian Club, the fabled San Francisco club started by writers and artists, in 1873, "but failed to qualify for non-payment of the initiation fee which was then $50.00." A pencil drawing, *Tommy Newcomb's Night*, was in the club collection in 1942.[7]

He may have revisited his home in Chicago in the summer of 1872. The Chicago Evening Journal of July 30, 1872, states that "Mr. Edwin Deakin, the artist, has just finished three pictures . . . the largest is a view of Lake Michigan . . . it is a work of great merit and justly places Mr. Deakin in the front ranks as a landscape painter."[8]

There is evidence that 1873 was a particularly busy year for Deakin. He advertised himself as a landscape painter in the May, 1873, issue of a sumptuous but short-lived publication, *The California Art Gallery*. His studio was given as 302 Montgomery,[9] which he occupied for some time.

He was in and around Cascade Lake and the Truckee River in fall of that year. (Cal. Mail Bag, Nov. 1873, Perret File). The *Gallery* reported, "Edwin Deakin has been industriously at work during the past two months producing several enjoyable pictures. The largest of these is a mellow representation of a view of the Rocky Mountains, at the source of the North Platte, showing the range of mountains with their snowcapped summits in the distance. The subject is well handled and there is some peculiarly good work in the foreground. At Morris, Schwab and Company, the same artist exhibits a pair of quiet studies—one of Lake Tahoe and the other of the Truckee Meadows. In quite another vein—and to us more satisfactory—are the two pictures which hang near; one, a view of the Old Mission church and the other a street in ancient London. Each subject is rich in suggestions and interesting by association, as well as intrinsically attractive, and the artist has also finished a view of Donner Lake, for the Bohemian Club, where it now hangs."[10]

The most revealing evidence of his art in these early years is a *Catalogue of a Special Artist's Sale* held May 21, 1873, with H. M. Newhall and Co. as auctioneers.[11] The catalogue announced "this elegant collection of Oil Paintings, all careful studies, highly finished, by Edwin Deakin, and handsomely framed in California Gold Frames, is now open for exhibition." Fifty-one paintings are listed, several of them apparently the same as those exhibited at Morris, Schwab & Company. While the list gives nothing but titles, it nevertheless is a clue to Deakin's work at the time, and gives us sufficient evidence to warrant some expanded general statements about his art—or at least about the subjects he portrayed.

Deakin was best known in these early years as a landscape painter. In fact, as we saw, he even advertised himself as such. A good half of the paintings in the 1873 Artist's Sale were landscapes. Of these, in turn about half were of California and half of other states. His California subjects included Donner Lake, Lake Tahoe, the Truckee River, the Yosemite, Mount Starr King, and other California-Nevada scenes.

Deakin's first recorded appearances as an exhibitor the previous year had also been as a landscapist. In the Arriola benefit exhibition in November he had shown *A View of the Truckee*.[12] For the December, 1872, exhibition of the San Francisco Art Association, "Edwin Deakin contributes his painting of the lower Yosemite Falls. The trees in the foreground are brought out in full detail, and the landscape well defined."[13] Throughout 1873, Deakin had apparently worked hard at landscape. "Deakin, the indefatigable, has returned from the mountains with fifty-five oil studies principally around Tallac Mountain and Lake Tahoe,"[14] one arti-

[6]*San Francisco Evening Bulletin*, December 6, 1872 and December 20, 1873 and from an invaluable card file on California artists prepared by Ferdinand Perret of Los Angeles. Original, Smithsonian Institution, copy, Oakland Art Museum. Referred to as *Perret File*.

[7]*Perret File*, op. cit.

[8]*Chicago Evening Journal*, July 30, 1872, Scrapbook Transcript. The date could be in error and refer to an event before his coming to San Francisco in 1870.

[9]*California Art Gallery*, 1873—no month given in Scrapbook Transcript; *S.F. City Directories* quoted in Perret Files.

[10]Ibid., *California Art Gallery*.

[11]*Catalogue of a Special Artist's Sale*, H. M. Newhall and Co., auctioneers, a copy in Bancroft Library, No. F870/A904, dated May 21, 1873.

[12]*San Francisco Chronicle*, November 15, 1872. Scrapbook Transcript.

[13]*San Francisco Daily Evening Bulletin*, December 6, 1872. Scrapbook Transcript.

[14]*San Francisco News Letter*, November 1, 1873. Scrapbook Transcript.

cle reported. Another writer commented on the results of this "protracted tour. There is an original style in Deakin's pictures—a mellow tone—a peaceful, pastoral sentiment pervading his landscapes; very restful and pleasing."[15] The landscape interest continued for some years. An 1874 article reports "Deakin spends four months out of every twelve, hunting the natural beauties of the Yosemite . . . he revels in purple tints and is considered the fastest worker in the city."[16] In 1876, it is reported that "(Samuel Marsden) Brookes and Deakin have returned from Mt. Shasta, and are hard at work upon the material obtained during their short trip. Deakin is at work upon a large picture of Shasta that gives an idea of the height and grandeur rarely seen anywhere but in nature."[17] Brookes, also an Englishman, and Deakin were close friends, and there are evidences that Brookes was occasionally influenced by Deakin's style of painting stone.[18] Deakin also did a charming painting in 1876, the year of their trip to Shasta together,[19] of Brookes at the easel in his dilapidated studio.

The landscapes in the 1873 exhibition also point out that Deakin by no means confined his activities to California. The subjects include the Green River in Wyoming, Lake Michigan, New York State, the Wasatch Mountains in Utah, scenes in Indiana and Illinois and a view on the Mississippi.

Deakin's interest in this kind of scenic painting declined throughout the 'seventies, and by the time of his return from a trip to Paris his interest in landscape was often confined to the background of his architectural pictures. We do not know the specific reasons which prompted Deakin's decision, but there were certainly adequate grounds. He was pitted against some of the most skillful technicians and honored talents painting in California, most of whom had discovered their subjects and had been exploiting them long before he arrived. Albert Bierstadt had already given California mountains his particular brand of heroic dramatization. That other Englishman, Thomas Hill, had already staked out his claim in the Yosemite Valley, and had advanced himself as its artist laureate. William Keith and many others were primarily occupied with landscapes. However well he might hold his own with at least the second string, the field was a bit crowded. Deakin had something more individual to contribute to California art, in another kind of subject.

The "Picturesque" in California

Deakin's main artistic accomplishment, of which we have evidence in the 1873 sale, was to establish a "Picturesque" style in California. In this new land, where the sensitive eye had seen local buildings only as one hasty rawness succeeding another, Deakin was able to find subjects which allowed him to conjure up nostalgic, sentimental visions giving California something of the mood of George Morland, Joseph Turner and Richard Bonington and their English castles, towns and cottages—buildings which he knew in his childhood and which he was to revisit later. The concept of the Picturesque is deeply imbedded in the popular imagination today—in fact, in a diluted and simplified way, it underlies the modern cult of the tourist attraction. It is difficult now to imagine there was ever a time here in California when the old missions, and San Francisco's Chinatown were not universally regarded as picturesque, but there was. These may have been historical curiosities, but the range of aesthetic response which finds such things quaint, nostalgic, and sentimental, which sees them as particularly fit subjects for pictures, would not exist without the concept of the Picturesque.

The idea of the Picturesque is an especially English development, and it is indicative of the cosmopolitan heritage of California that a young man of English background should have brought it here. By the time Deakin had begun his career as an artist, the Picturesque style had been in existence for half a century. More sophisticated English and European artists had found new enthusiasms by this time, but there was still an increasing audience for it in less avant-garde circles. The Picturesque style, essentially Romantic in nature, had begun with the first years of the nineteenth century. It was interjected as a third alternative to Burke's con-

[15]*Daily Alta California*, November 9, 1873. Scrapbook Transcript.

[16]*San Francisco Chronicle*, June 22, 1874. Scrapbook Transcript.

[17]*San Francisco Chronicle*, October 30, 1876. Scrapbook Transcript.

[18]*Samuel Marsden Brookes*, California Historical Society and Oakland Art Museum exhibition catalogue edited by Joseph Armstrong Baird, Jr., 1962-3. *Cock Fight*, Catalog No. 2.

[19]Ibid., De Young Museum, No. 108.

cepts of the Beautiful and the Sublime, and it opposed the basically Neo-Classicist tastes of the day. Ruins, old castles, quaint country cottages, old twisted trees, storms, waterfalls, ancient towns and streets, the daily lives of gypsies, country folk,—in fact, everything irregular and unusual by virtue of not being in itself the Beautiful—was found to be a source of aesthetic pleasure.

Deakin apparently became interested in the "Picturesque" during his youth in England, and whatever his training in this country might have been, it encouraged him in this direction. If he first emphasized his talents as a landscape painter when he arrived in California, nevertheless he had also cultivated his taste for the "Picturesque" from the beginning.

The 1873 sale contained at least seven Picturesque European subjects, and the three California mission paintings. The European subjects are patently Picturesque, even if we know only the titles. Most are English views: *Ancient London*, *Old English Abbey*, *Dudley Castle—Staffordshire*, and *An English Lane*. There are also views of Strasburg and Antwerp, the last subtitled *Procession—an Old Street View*.

It is a little difficult to account for the existence of these European subjects. Deakin's first documented return to Europe was about 1877. Consequently, these paintings must be based on sketches made prior to his departure at the age of 18, or have resulted from another trip we know nothing about, or, perhaps, be based on engravings without direct observation on Deakin's part at all. At any rate, European subjects were second only to landscape in Deakin's attention even at this early time. He continued to paint them regularly throughout the rest of his life.

What interests us more is his picturesque portrayal of the California missions. These are first known to have been exhibited in the 1873 "Artist's Sale," but we have some earlier evidence of his interest in the subject, and of course considerable material from later years. Let us consider the entire topic of Deakin and the missions at this point.

Deakin and the Missions

Deakin apparently responded to the picturesque appeal of the missions immediately upon his arrival in California. Other than landscapes, Mission Dolores seems to be his first California subject. He later noted that he had begun making "sketches and studies" of Mission Dolores in 1870, the year of his arrival,[20] and there are pencil sketches of the mission in the Howard Willoughby's collection dated that year. The three paintings he exhibited in the 1873 sale are titled *The Old Mission, San Francisco*, *Mansion House—Part of the Old Mission*, and *Mission Dolores, San Francisco*. (Picturesque art could hardly do without the adjective "old"; its appearance in a title is almost always an indication of an underlying picturesque concept.)

He apparently did not pursue the depiction of the missions for several years, during which time we know him to have been busy as a landscape painter. He sketched Mission San Buenaventura and Mission Santa Ines in 1875, he states, and the rest of the existing missions between the years 1878 and 1899. Three of the missions had been wholly destroyed. He notes that "the outlines of Santa Clara Mission were obtained from a daguerreotype taken about 1855. The outlines of the Santa Cruz Mission, now extinct, are taken from an old painting by L. Tousset." He gives acknowledgment "To Mr. Watkins for use of photograph of Mission San José, taken before the earthquake of 1868, and another of the corridor of Mission San Luis Obispo. To Mr. William J. Miller for full description of Mission San Rafael, now extinct . . ." He also notes, "Of the three missions that are wholly destroyed, careful studies of the sites have been made."

Deakin produced several kinds of paintings of the missions. In addition to his working sketches, almost all of which are in the Howard Willoughby collection in the Oakland Art Museum, there are many paintings. A number of the paintings are conceived as individual compositions, and vary considerably in format and in the kind of accompanying detail and foreground material. No attempt has been made to catalogue these, and they are to be found in various collections throughout the state. Next, there are three complete series of paintings of the twenty-one missions. Two of these series are large oil paintings. They are nearly identical. One of these series is the one now in the Los Angeles County Museum of Natural History. It came to them about 1930. The other series was in Edwin Deakin's own estate and remained

13

[20]Deakin, *The Twenty-One Missions of California*, reproduced from paintings by Deakin, Berkeley, 1900, Foreword.

in storage until brought to light by Howard Willoughby. This series was presented by Mr. and Mrs. Willoughby to the Franciscan Fathers to be displayed at Mission Santa Barbara, in the Willoughby's original home town. Whichever is the second set, it was undertaken as insurance against inadvertent loss in such disasters as the fires which scourged bay area cities and, among other treasures, destroyed thousands of works of art.

The artist also did a series of small watercolors, eight and one-half inches by eleven and one-half inches, of the same compositions. These brilliant little watercolors were executed to have been reproduced in a book on the missions. Deakin also did a map and decorations for the book, including his coat of arms. Deakin was evidently very proud of this coat of arms, for he used it repeatedly, even stencilling it on the back of some of his paintings. The watercolors had been in storage with the Deakin estate. They had been sewn into a canvas bag for protection, and are still as fresh and crisp as the day they were painted.

Artistically, the three series have similar characteristics. The compositions were arranged to show as much of each mission, including its church facade, as possible. Each is depicted against its natural setting. Some of the other individual paintings of the missions, showing only portions of a building, have more interest as compositions, but Deakin's intention in the series was to record the whole. In style, they can only be described as early Turneresque. Joseph Turner's views of English country seats, or similar views, must have been somewhat in the back of Deakin's mind. Many of the California hillsides in the backgrounds show wisps of fog trailing across them. The trails of mist and fog were always favorite motifs of Deakin, and they were also a characteristic device of Turner, who enlivened the backgrounds of his views with great wraiths of fog draped across English hillsides. The watercolor series is, incidentally, done on a fine grade of English watercolor paper, with a surprisingly heavy tooth, considering the size of the carefully detailed nature of the paintings.

Deakin did, indeed, publish his book of reproductions of the missions, though not in as lavish a form as the watercolor series indicates he had in mind. It is, in fact, a simple publication, with rather small black-and-white reproductions and hardly more than a foreword and a list of the missions for a text. It was published in Berkeley in 1900, and had been copyrighted by Deakin in 1899. He exhibited his mission collection at the Palace Hotel in San Francisco in 1899 and again in 1900.

Deakin and the California missions received a great deal of attention in the early years of this century. A considerable movement, especially among women's groups, was on foot to restore the missions and El Camino Real, which linked them. Deakin is credited as having done much to arouse this interest. Several magazine articles appeared on his work and on the mission restoration project. An article titled "The Painter of the California Missions" appeared in *The Outlook* in January of 1904, written by Pauline R. Bird. "Edwin Deakin has opened the eyes of California to the urgency of preserving these landmarks and to this end the Road (El Camino Real) will doubtless be restored and preserved," she wrote. "To Edwin Deakin, the 'artist-historian,' is directly due the inspiration of the many clubs . . . that are today enthusiastically taking up the subject of the opening and restoring of El Camino Real."[21]

In *Brush and Pencil* a year later, Robert L. Hewitt wrote of Deakin's paintings under the rather distressing title, "Edwin Deakin, An Artist with a Mission." All his information about Deakin appears to have been taken from the 1900 book. Hewitt's comments further define the concepts underlying the picturesque response to the missions. "It was a happy thought to undertake the task of transmitting to future generations these notable old structures in all their time-worn beauty, . . ." he says. "It will readily be seen that the interest of the canvases is largely historical, and yet the crumbling condition of many of the structures and their unusual style of architecture lend them an air of the picturesque that is wholly wanting in many of the paintings the scenes of which have been carefully selected by artists for their intrinsic grandeur or beauty. Few of the localities selected as sketching-grounds by artists have the atmospheric beauties of California, and when to this is added the fact that some of these buildings date back to the middle of the eighteenth century and are stained and mellowed by time and crumbling into ruins it can easily be understood

[21]*The Outlook*, op. cit.

that the missions were subjects to delight the heart of a true painter."[22]

Deakin was not the first American artist to complete a series on the missions. Henry Chapman Ford's series of etchings were published in 1883. Many artists did a few missions, without completing the series, among them William Keith, who had sketched them on his honeymoon in the same year, 1883, and painted a few of them some years later. Other artists did mission series after Deakin's. However, Deakin was the first to begin a series which was brought to a successful completion. In 1904, Deakin was still thinking of extending his coverage of Spanish colonial buildings to other states. Pauline R. Bird said, "Mr. Deakin's work is far from being finished. He hopes and expects to paint the Jesuit Missions of southern California and probably also even those of Arizona and Mexico."[23] These views, however, were never to materialize.

Deakin's artistic career was by no means confined to the missions. He pursued the picturesque down many paths both here and in Europe. Let us retrace our steps, and briefly indicate the other significant events in Deakin's career as an artist.

Work in Europe

From 1878 to 1880 Deakin returned to Europe, visiting both England and France. He did a number of sketches and paintings of such English monuments as Westminster Abbey and Stoke Poges, picking such romantic spots as the Poets' Corner, and an extensive series of sketches and paintings in France. Various views of Notre Dame and the Seine, Cluny, Clamart, Gentilly, resulted from this visit. He also travelled to Mont Blanc and to Lake Chillon in Switzerland, whose fabled Castle and the Dent du Midi were favorite subjects. A charming collection of European sketches, mostly from the year 1878, is in the Oakland Art Museum collection, the gift of Mr. and Mrs. Don Grenier. Deakin used these sketches as the source of many paintings completed in later years in the United States, and prized certain of his European paintings as among his best, including them in "the Deakin Collection" he wanted kept intact, now the property of the State of California and deposited with the Oakland Art Museum. Two of these paintings, *Mont Blanc* and *L'Eglise de Chelles La Soir*, were exhibited in the 1879 Salon in Paris, adding a note of prestige to his career which was important through the rest of his life. He is also supposed to have exhibited at the Luxembourg Gallery and at the Royal Academy in London.[24]

California Again

Back in California, we next hear of him through an auction sale of paintings in 1881. Deakin had regular recourse to auction sales as a source of funds; in 1875 he had sold 71 studies from nature for a total of $4500;[25] in the 1881 sale he netted only $2500 for a group of "oil paintings" auctioned in the rooms of the San Francisco Art Association.[26] As was usually the case, he put a high reserve on certain paintings, and withdrew them for lack of a sufficient bid.

In 1882 and 1883 he was in Denver, Colorado, with his family. He was quite the artistic lion. A Denver journalist[27] deemed him ". . . the best artist who has ever visited Denver. He has made more of a success in art than perhaps any other artist who has ever been here." Governor Grant was among the purchasers of his work. "It is a pleasure to visit his studio," the writer reported. "The placard on the door looks uninviting. It says in fierce black letters, 'Engaged till 4 o'clock.' If you happen to be a friend and know the signal knock, you are admitted out of hours. He greets you pleasantly and makes you welcome. His studio is full of beautiful paintings, foreign and native landscapes and print pictures. There are woodland scenes, flocks and their shepherds, old inns, romantic chateaux, rustic bridges and mountain scenes with lakes of clear crystal water and picturesque old mills. Standing by itself upon a large easel, draped with a crimson cloth, is a picture which is a masterpiece. It

[22]*Brush and Pencil*, Vol. XV, No. 1, January 1905, "Edwin Deakin, An Artist with a Mission" by Robert L. Hewitt.

[23]*The Outlook*, op. cit.

[24]Howard Willoughby letter, op. cit.

[25]*Alta California*, February 25, 1875, page 1, col. 3.

[26]*Alta California*, October 27, 1881, page 1, col. 4.

[27]*San Francisco Call*, April 9, 1883 (reprint from Denver paper).

is a painting of the interior of Westminster Abbey, taken from the choir. The light falls sidewise across the picture coming from the poet's corner. The scene is the throne where the kings and queens of England are crowned. The observer can fancy he stands looking into the church itself, and the illusion is wonderfully perfect. The painting is quite large, and when properly framed—that is with doors to close and a flight of steps leading up—will be a magnificent ornament for a hall or picture gallery. The work is masterly; the marble floor, the stone pillars, the painted glass window, the dim religious light, are marvelous. It is a wonder of perspective. Mr. Deakin never neglects the slightest detail in a picture. The chain of the gas chandelier hangs from the ceiling, but is so lost in shadow and light that it appears only here and there, and the picture is not marred by one long straight line. The reporter bids good morning to Mr. Deakin, feeling that Denver will 'never see his like again.'"

(The celebrated Westminster Abbey painting continued to be one of his *chef d'oeuvre*. It had been offered but withdrawn in the 1881 sale. In the 1884 sale, "The auctioneer talked for half an hour in an endeavor to raise the bid . . . on the famous picture of 'Westminster Abbey' . . . but not being successful the painting was withdrawn by the artist's authority, he having been offered $2000 for it in the East." The present whereabouts of the painting is not known.)

Deakin returned to San Francisco in June of 1883. Another auction sale was held in October, 1884.[28] Eighty paintings were offered, including every kind of work; European and American subjects, landscapes, architectural pieces and still life paintings. Reported prices ranged from $125 to $280. In these years, Deakin developed the second of his major picturesque subjects, San Francisco's Chinatown. Though it had been painted before, Deakin's paintings, most dated in the late 'eighties, caught the particular charm and appeal of the crowded alleys and their exotic residents as no painter has before or since.

In 1890, Deakin purchased a part of what had been the Peralta Estate in Berkeley, bounded by Telegraph Avenue, present-day Deakin Street, Webster and Woolsey Streets. He built a mission-style studio there, and did a number of sketches of the surrounding meadows and hills, most dated 1894, which are among the earliest views of Berkeley.

Another auction was held in December, 1893.[29] It was less of a success. *The Cathedral of Notre Dame, Paris*, valued at $5,000, was sold to Mrs. Remi Chabot of Oakland for $400. (The painting is now in the Oakland Art Museum, the gift of her daughter and son-in-law, Mr. and Mrs. Leon Chabot Bocqueraz.) The auctioneer complained, "We are giving these pictures away, it would be as well to throw them into the street and have done with it." Other paintings, including some now in the state collection, were withdrawn, but nevertheless a great number were sold.

As we saw earlier, the turn of the century was marked by Deakin's completion of the mission series, its exhibition in the Palace Hotel in 1899 and 1900, the publication of his book of reproductions of the mission paintings, and his emergence as an initiator and leader of the movement to save the missions and El Camino Real. It also resulted in the articles on the missions and his work.

Later Years

The 1906 earthquake and fire for some time redirected the course of Deakin's work. He did a series of four views showing San Francisco in flames, as seen at night from Berkeley; small and sketch-like as they are, they have an urgency and poignancy which few other fire paintings have. Deakin and certain other artists suddenly discovered in ruined San Francisco a "picturesque" subject of the sort they had found only in Europe and seldom on this continent. A series of sketches and paintings came from Deakin's hands; *Despair*, showing the ruined city from Nob Hill; the desolate grounds of the Mark Hopkins house, and other subjects.

His missions continued to attract press attention, however. In 1908, Lucy B. Jerome wrote of them on display in his Berkeley studio, and reported, "the artist has a plan for the restoration of the Mission Dolores, which is worthy of the source of its inspiration and which he hopes to see

---

[28] *San Francisco Call*, October 3, 1884, page 3, col. 8.
[29] *San Francisco Chronicle*, December 8, 1893, page 4, col. 3.

carried out before he dies." She concluded with, "it has been said that Deakin paints in a style of twenty years ago, but putting style aside anyone who can behold the picturing of the lovely, shadowy arched missions unmoved has the soul of a stoic."[30]

California provided Deakin with one last picturesque subject before his death. In the Panama Pacific International Exposition of 1915-1916, the center of attraction was Bernard Maybeck's Palace of Fine Arts. A personal interpretation of a neo-classic rotunda flanked by a pillared arcade, reflected in a romantic lagoon and overgrown with trees and bushes, it consciously recalled the ruined grandeurs depicted by Piranesi. It was a Deakin subject, and Deakin painted it, if with faltering and less sure hand, several times.

Deakin died in Berkeley on May 11, 1923, nearly 85 years old, survived by his widow, Isabel, and his daughters, Edna and Dorothy. He had lived beyond his time and his companions. The San Francisco Chronicle called him "the last member of a group of celebrated painters of early San Francisco days."[31]

The bulk of his collection, including a number of his more prized works, was put in storage, and remained there for many years. His work in behalf of the missions was forgotten, and recalled. *Flaming Tokay*, 1884, in the De Young Museum collection—one of the grape paintings which were another specialty of his throughout his life—was exhibited in the Golden Gate International Exposition on Treasure Island in 1940 in an exhibition titled "California Art in Retrospect—1850-1915."[32] In 1947, a bill was presented to the California State Senate Finance Committee to purchase for the state the collection of mission paintings "at present housed in the vaults of the Los Angeles County Museum,"[33] but it failed to pass.

Today, Deakin is sharing with other California painters, long forgotten in our neglect of the artists of our own past, a new and important place. The revival of Deakin is due principally to Howard Willoughby, who in 1951 discovered the existence of the Deakin Collection in storage, and acquired it from the Deakin estate. Most of the paintings from this collection are, through his efforts, now in the Oakland Art Museum's collection of California art, the principal collection in this field. Also a pioneer in the Deakin revival were Miss Ruth Mahood, Chief Curator of History, and the staff of the History Division of the Los Angeles County Museum of Natural History, who revived, acquired and restored the great series of oil paintings of the missions, now such an ornament to their exhibition halls, and in 1960 presented the first museum-sponsored one-man exhibition of his work since his death. The issuance of this publication is further evidence of their continuing devotion to the work of Deakin and of California's early artists.

PAUL MILLS
Curator Oakland Art Museum

[30]*San Francisco Call*, July 12, 1908, page 29, col. 1.
[31]*San Francisco Chronicle*, May 27, 1923.
[32]*Perret File*, op. cit.
[33]*The Argonaut*, May 30, 1947, page 4.

Mission San Diego de Alcala

In San Diego, as its citizens like to point out, "California began." It was at Point Loma, in 1542, that Juan Rodriguez Cabrillo first discovered the California coast. And it was at San Diego on July 16, 1769 that Father Junípero Serra, padre-presidente of the missions, founded the Franciscan mission that became the first European settlement in California. It was named for St. Didacus (San Diego) of Alcala, Spain, who was born of lowly parents near Seville, and died at Alcala on November 12, 1463, revered for the miracles he is said to have performed.

From Old Town, where it was first established, the mission was moved, in 1774, to Mission Valley, seven miles northwest of San Diego's present civic center, where it now stands. On November 4 and 5, 1775, some 800 Indians attacked the mission by night, and several defenders were killed or injured. Martyred at that time was Father Jayme, who cried out to his attackers, as they killed him, "Love God, my children." Father Junípero Serra, it is said, declared that the land had been watered with the blood of martyrs and so was sanctified.

After the attack the mission was rebuilt, but it was difficult to get converts for some time. However, in 1824, there were 1,829 Indian neophytes at the mission.

The present church was built between 1808 and 1813. After secularization of the missions in 1834, the buildings began slowly to fall into ruin. By the end of the century little more than the chapel remained, and it was badly dilapidated, the bell tower having fallen. In 1931, the church was restored and the belfry rebuilt. The façade of the church is the most interesting feature.

This mission is located five miles east of State Highway 5 in Mission Valley, off State Highway 8.

The Mission of San Carlos Borromeo de Carmelo (Carmel)

San Carlos Borromeo, named for St. Charles Borromeo, a Cardinal of the 16th century, was the mother mission, the headquarters of the Franciscans in Alta California, and the "home" of Father Junípero Serra, who died there in 1784. He was buried in the church. Monterey Bay was chosen even before California was settled to become the capital of Spanish California, and so it was that Carmel Mission (so-called for the Carmel River) became the second mission, founded June 3, 1770. Father Serra moved the mission from its original site at Monterey to Carmel, four miles south on the Bay of Monterey, 1771, because of the presence of water (Carmel River), irrigable land and a number of Indian villages. All of which were lacking at Monterey.

The present stone church was constructed between 1793 and 1797 by Father Lasuén, and dedicated in 1797. The columns on either side of the door, the arches, and unique Moorish tower all impress visitors. Although no vestige of the original roof now remains, it had an elliptical vault and curved walls. Thus the nave of the church was curiously oval-shaped. It has been restored. The Moorish star window has been called by Rexford Newcomb the richest ornament at San Carlos; it is made from a combination of circle and square.

By 1836, however, San Carlos was a ruin, and in 1852 the roof crashed. Some with romantic inclinations assert that Joaquin Murietta used to lurk about the ruins. More prosaically, squatters took over the mission, but they were ejected by President Buchanan's patent to the Catholic Church on October 19, 1859. Father Angelo D. Casanova, rector of Monterey Parish, arrived in 1870 with the intention of reviving the grand days of Father Serra. He raised funds, removed debris, reroofed the mission church, and found the graves of Father Serra and three other pioneer Franciscans. July 3, 1882 was a dramatic day at Carmel. Four hundred people witnessed the removal of the redwood coffins containing the remains of the padres. This quieted rumors that the bodies of Serra, Crespí, and Lasuén had been stolen. The graves were closed and, today, marble slabs in the sanctuary mark the graves of Serra and his colleagues.

Soon, a thorough restoration was undertaken. The shingle roof of Father Casanova was replaced, in 1936, with a low-pitched tile one. The monastery buildings, which had entirely disintegrated, were rebuilt. Harry Downie, after long hours of research, realistically restored Father Serra's cell. It contains his Latin Bible, some of the original floor tiles, and the mood of the room in which California's founder died.

Carmel Mission is located just south of the City of Carmel, near State Highway 1.

Mission San Antonio de Padua

In an oak glen through which the San Antonio River flows southeastwardly to join the Salinas stands California's third mission, San Antonio de Padua. Its founding occurred on July 14, 1771, when an Indian happened by as Father Serra was saying Mass. Serra caressed the man and gave him gifts—and a new mission was born. It is poetic justice that more than a century and a half later, Doña Perfecta Encinal, a descendant of the early Indian converts, brought her sons, daughters, and grandchildren to labor on the mission's restoration.

Between 1810 and 1813, the present church of brick and adobe rose. It possesses a fine façade with curved gable and low bell towers. Rexford Newcomb, an architect who wrote, in 1925, THE OLD MISSION CHURCHES AND HISTORIC HOUSES OF CALIFORNIA, said that in some ways this was the most beautiful curved gable at any mission. It is unique in that it was built in two stages, the upper of which is pierced by a central arch and flanked by low arch-pierced towers. In 1903, due to the interest created by the Honorable Joseph R. Knowland, the California Historic Landmarks League was formed to restore the missions. San Antonio was the first mission chosen for this restoration. After several years of difficulties, such as heavy rains in 1904-1905, an earthquake in 1906, and muddy roads in 1907, restoration of the church was finally completed. Then in 1948-49, the church, which was in a shambles, was almost completely restored, as was much of the mission compound.

San Antonio was famous for its flour, known throughout California. One may still see the flour mill, now reconstructed. This stone mill was operated by water brought for many miles through a stonewalled ditch or *zanja*.

Newcomb's impressions of the locality is expressed in these words from his book: "A drowsy May day in this beautiful valley is one of life's real experiences. Nature has her own way; silence, complete except for the twitting of the birds, reigns supreme; even the breeze is stilled."

San Antonio Mission is located off U.S. Highway 101, 27 miles northwest of Bradley, or 23 miles southwest of King City.

Mission San Gabriel Arcángel

San Gabriel was the fourth mission established in Alta California. On September 8, 1771, it was founded by Fathers Pedro Benito Cambón and Angel Somera. Being on the direct overland route from Mexico to Monterey, San Gabriel was the stopping place and first supply station for wayfarers who had crossed the perilous desert and mountains. Here came such historic figures as Juan Bautista de Anza, the trail-blazer, and rugged beaver-trapping mountain men, including Jedediah Strong Smith and Ewing Young. Here also ended the famous Old Spanish Trail, a mule-caravan route between Santa Fe and Los Angeles in the Mexican Era. Always historically important, San Gabriel became, in 1831, a hospital after a battle between Governor José Echeandía and his successor, Manuel Victoria.

The mission had moved from its original site, which was five miles south of the present one, on a bluff overlooking Rio Hondo. Floods forced the Franciscan padres to make this move in 1775. They chose higher land in very fertile country. Under exceptional leadership even for Franciscans, San Gabriel rapidly became one of the wealthiest of missions. Grapes, olives, oranges, figs, and pears flourished, while herds of cattle and flocks of sheep multiplied.

Built in 1791-1805, under Father José Mariá Zalvidea, the present church is of stone and cement as far as the windows, with brick above, to lighten the load against earthquake shocks. This mission appears more like a fortress than any other, due to its massive walls and flying buttresses and because the windows are placed high. Its stark simplicity is relieved by an outside stairway to the choir loft and a belfry with several arches interestingly cut to correspond to the different sizes of the bells. The church was damaged by earthquake in 1812 and repaired in 1828.

Secularization was begun in 1834. Actually San Gabriel was never abandoned with regard to religious worship and the records show continuity of pastors. The last Franciscans left in 1851 and were immediately replaced by pastors working under a bishop. In 1859, the property was given to two Americans to settle a debt, but also in 1859, the United States Land Commission declared the sale invalid and returned San Gabriel to the Catholic Church. Today, it is the property of the Claretean Fathers who have preserved it well.

San Gabriel Mission is located in the city of San Gabriel on Mission Drive, about nine miles east of downtown Los Angeles.

The Mission San Luis Obispo de Tòlosa

Father Junípero Serra, assisted by Father José Cavaller, founded this fifth California mission on September 1, 1772 and named it for St. Louis, young Bishop of Toulouse, France. Son of King Charles II of Naples and nephew of Louis IX of France, he had become a Franciscan in 1294.

To Father Luis Antonio Martínez, who in 1798 began a long term of service there, goes credit for the mission's real prosperity. It is said that he did engage in smuggling in 1830. This was because very few supplies came directly from Mexico and it was simpler and more sensible to trade with Yankee ships which frequented the coast. Martínez was undoubtedly a frank, fearless, extroverted man, and a canny businessman. Fr. Martínez' superior said he had the best managed mission.

Though never one of the most prosperous missions, San Luis Obispo's history was far from uneventful. Pagan Indians set fire to outlying buildings. The area was overrun by bears.

The present mission church was built in 1793. Inside the edifice the open-timber roof was marred by the boarding up of the under side of the beams. But this was a godsend in a sense, because later it prevented the original beams from being burned during a severe fire. Recently, the history-minded restorers of San Luis Obispo have returned the mission to its original appearance. The colonnaded portico and the arched narthex have been rebuilt.

This mission is located at the corner of Monterey and Chorro Streets in downtown San Luis Obispo, a city on U.S. Highway 101.

Mission of San Francisco de Asis ("Dolores")

Saint Francis is said to be the world's most popular saint. He was born in 1182 in Assisi, the son of Pietro Bernardone, a rich cloth merchant. Francis passed a worldly youth, but eventually renounced his inheritance, put on beggar's garments, kissed lepers' sores, and lived in a cave. His love for all living things is proverbial. He died on October 4, 1226, after he had founded the Franciscan Order.

The Mission of San Francisco is also popularly called "Dolores," because of a little rivulet nearby (now gone) which was named by Captain Juan Bautista de Anza, who led the first colonizing expedition to San Francisco in 1776. He called the rivulet "Dolores" because he discovered it on the day of The Feast of Our Lady of Sorrows, the Friday before Holy Week. Anza also chose the site for the mission. The mission, California's sixth, was formally founded on October 9, 1776.

Temporary wooden buildings with thatched roofs were used until the church, begun in 1782, was completed—sometime before 1795. Although most California missions suffered from the earthquake of 1812, the one at San Francisco was spared and is still intact today.

In 1849 gold seekers squatted on the mission lands. In 1850 a plank toll road connected the growing city of San Francisco with the old mission where omnibuses ran every half hour. On Saturday nights fandangos were held at the once quiet mission, and several saloons and two race tracks were found nearby. Also, Lola Montez married editor, Patrick Hull, at the mission.

When the great earthquake of April 18, 1906, hit San Francisco, the modern church which stood beside the old adobe mission crumbled, but not the church of the padres! Its adobe bricks seemed to "sway" with the tremors and thus withstood the shocks. The flames of the fire which followed the quake stopped just one block away.

In 1917 Monsignor John W. Sullivan began restoration work with the aid of architect, Willis Polk. Steel beams were placed in grooves on the exterior of the adobe walls, and the space was filled and covered with cement so that the beams inside and out were invisible. Steel trestles were used to support the heavy roof.

Today, thousands of visitors annually visit the chapel and the interesting little cemetery beside it, where they enjoy its massive simplicity, which is always impressive.

Mission "Dolores" is located in San Francisco on Dolores Street, between 16th and 17th Streets, three blocks south of Market Street.

San Juan Capistrano Mission

San Juan Capistrano, the seventh mission founded in California, was named for St. John of Capistrano, an Italian theologian and one of the few lawyers ever canonized. An attempt to establish a mission on this spot in October, 1775, was abandoned because of an Indian attack on the San Diego mission. But on October 30, 1776, the missionaries arrived again, disinterred the bells they had buried for safekeeping, and refounded the mission. November 1, 1776, is recorded as the date of its formal establishment.

In 1797 a great stone church was begun, the finest building architecturally ever built by Spain in California. Isidoro Aguilar, a master stonemason from Culiacán, Mexico, supervised the construction and the stonecutting. Sandstone was quarried and transported by oxen six miles from the northeast. The building was designed in the shape of a Latin Cross, covered with seven low domes of stone, one of which can still be seen over the ruined sanctuary. On September 7, 1806, the governor attended the dedication of the church.

On December 8, 1812, during the Feast of the Immaculate Conception, an earthquake shook the church while Mass was being held. Thirty-nine neophytes were killed.

The church was never rebuilt. The bells were hung in a new *campanario*, where they may still be seen. The present "Serra's church," where the chapel is located, is California's oldest building and the only one in which Father Junípero Serra himself held services.

In 1818 pirate Hippolyte Bouchard raided the mission but only burned some straw houses and stole some wine.

After the Mexican government secularized the missions, Capistrano declined rapidly. In 1895 the Landmarks Club of Los Angeles preserved some of the walls and reroofed a portion of the cloisters. At that time the church was being used as a lumber warehouse.

On Easter Sunday, April 20, 1924, Mass was said in Serra's church for the first time in several decades. Father O'Sullivan, who since 1910 had contributed so much time and effort to the reconstruction of San Juan Capistrano, also recreated the mission garden, where he was buried after his death in July, 1933.

This mission is located in San Juan Capistrano on Interstate Highway 5.

Mission Santa Clara de Asis

The site of Santa Clara Mission is on the present campus of the University of Santa Clara, about forty-five miles southeast of San Francisco. It was named for Clara of Assisi, who at seventeen was touched by the spirit of St. Francis of her own city. Clara was a beautiful girl of the upper classes, and Francis was skeptical at first of her devotion. He tested it by having her dress in sackcloth and beg alms for the poor before her own father's door. She did this and also sheared off her hair and took vows of poverty, chastity, and obedience in 1212. For forty years she spread the teachings of Saint Francis.

The mission was founded under Junípero Serra's presidency by Padre Tomás de la Peña, January 12, 1777. The first site was abandoned because of floods, but the permanent church was built between 1781 and 1784 and designed by Padre Murguía, who died four days before the dedication. In the earthquake of 1812, which wrecked so many mission structures, the church fell. A new one, built between 1817 and 1822, was used as a college chapel until it was destroyed by fire. Today, only a remnant of the adobe cloisters remains, at the rear of the new university chapel, patterned after the last mission church.

From the beginning, Santa Clara Valley was a garden spot, surpassed only by that of San Gabriel. The first fruits offered by California to the forty-niners were grapes and pears from the mission orchards of Santa Clara and San José. By 1800, Santa Clara had a larger Indian population than any mission in California—2228. There was drama at Santa Clara, too. In 1839 the mission was the scene of a great social event, the wedding of Governor Juan Bautista Alvarado and Doña Martina Castro. Alvarado, though tremendously able, was a scandalously dissolute man, who had left the mother of his illegitimate children to marry Martina. Even so, Alvarado did not appear at his own wedding, but was married in absentia, represented by his brother-in-law. Later, he welcomed his bride at Monterey.

In March, 1851, the Santa Clara College was established at the mission by Father John Nobili. In 1926 the mission building and some relics were destroyed by fire. The new building has some of the tiles from the former church which had been taken down and stored away.

It is located in Santa Clara, on the Alameda.

The Mission of San Buenaventura

This, the ninth California mission, was founded March 31, 1782, the last to be established by Father Junípero Serra. It was named for John Fidanza, born in Tuscany in 1221. It is said that he was restored to health by Saint Francis who exclaimed "O buona ventura," (oh, good fortune!). From this John Fidanza got his religious name, "Buonaventura" in Italian. Due to the highly populous Indian settlements in the area, Serra had long wanted a mission there; but the founding was delayed by many factors, and once the first buildings were erected, they were destroyed by fire. The present adobe church, begun in 1793, was completed by 1809, damaged by the famous earthquake of 1812, and later repaired. Today it is the only mission building still standing. The side doorway is the most interesting feature; it is a Moorish arch flanked by stone pilasters.

Although for a long time there were very few baptisms at San Buenaventura, the area soon prospered agriculturally. Ironically, in 1800, the mission raised more grain and cattle than any other mission but had the smallest population of neophytes. The mission gardens were famous and were mentioned in the writings of George Vancouver, the British Navy officer who visited California in the 1790's. Richard Henry Dana, Jr. as late as the 1830's called these gardens the finest in California.

Nevertheless, secularization was costly to the mission. After another devastating earthquake, in 1857, the church remained roofless for years. Finally it was remodeled in the 'nineties, but so badly that it resembled a Victorian-style church more than a mission, and many of the Indian art works were destroyed. Fortunately, it has been repaired since then. A high hill behind the mission was chosen for a cross and called "La Loma de la Cruz." The original cross is gone, but has been replaced. In pioneer days the cross could be seen for miles.

In 1888, the town which had grown up about the mission had its name shortened to "Ventura."

San Buenaventura Mission is located in the city of Ventura, just east of U.S. Highway 101.

Santa Barbara, tenth of the California missions founded by the Franciscan fathers, is one of the best preserved and finest architecturally. Because of the populous Chumash tribe along the coast, Father Junípero Serra longed to found a mission in this area. A presidio was established April 21, 1782. The site chosen for the mission was about three-quarters of a league from the army post. Called "El Pedregoso" (Rocky Mound) for its stony soil, the imposing spot was at the foot of the Santa Ines Mountains.

Because of Serra's death in 1784, the mission was actually founded by his successor, Father Fermín Francisco de Lasuén, who performed the ceremonies of consecration on December 16, 1786. Nevertheless, the Day of Saint Barbara, December 4, has always been regarded as its founding date since that was the date Father Lasuén first raised the cross and blessed it. Saint Barbara, according to legend, was a third-century Roman maiden of Asia Minor who, at seventeen, was tortured and killed by her own pagan father because she would not abjure Christianity. She is the protectress against thunder, lighting, and sudden death, for it is said that a thunderbolt struck her father dead!

In 1787 the first temporary chapel, dwellings, and storehouses were begun while converts slowly increased. By 1807 there were over 1700 neophytes. The first church of wood and thatch was replaced in 1789 by one of adobe, only to be superseded in 1793-94 by a larger church. After the damaging quake of 1812, a fourth structure was erected and dedicated September 10, 1820. It has been repaired many times but still stands. Major reconstruction was done after the June, 1925 temblor (when one tower fell), and again in 1950-53. Its walls are six feet thick and of native sandstone. Solid stone buttresses eight feet thick support this most solidly built of missions. The design was taken by Father Antonio Ripoll from a work of architecture by the Roman, Vitruvius Pollio, thus the ornate façade.

The mission is also noted for its double-tiered fountain, often copied, and the largest remaining at any mission. Its garden and cemetery are famous.

Santa Barbara Mission was never surrendered by the Franciscan Order. In 1853 a petition to Rome resulted in its being established as a hospice, the beginning of its role as an apostolic college for the education of Franciscan missionaries. It became the mother house of the modern Franciscan Province, where the archives of the California missions are preserved, and at the same time is a Franciscan theological seminary. Here visitors may see many fine relics. Helen Hunt Jackson called it a "benediction on the whole city"; modern Barbareños and visitors alike agree.

The mission is located in the city of Santa Barbara at the end of Laguna Street.

La Purísima Concepción, the eleventh mission, founded in Alta, California was established on December 2, 1787 by Father-President Fermín de Lasuén, to serve the thickly populated Santa Barbara Channel coast. La Purísima Concepción never was one of the most important missions and its architecture was without real distinction. Purísima's history was turbulent. On December 21, 1812, the great earthquake split Mission Hill in two, and the results may still be seen. Rebellion flared at Purísima Concepción in 1824, but it was put down. Seven Indians were executed for the uprising in spite of the padre's efforts to save them.

In the 1850's, the frontier desperado, Jack Powers, led his lawless band of five from the environs of Purísima Concepción to prey on travelers between San Luis Obispo and Santa Barbara. Powers had originally been a member of Colonel John Stevenson's regiment which came to California during the Mexican War. A short, dark-haired, bearded man, resembling a Spanish Californian, he assumed the manners of a ranchero and excelled in gambling and dancing. Later, Powers came to a bad end, killed by his own men in Mexico. About that time, the mission buildings sank to ignominious uses, serving as stables and sheepfolds.

By the end of the century, the mission was gradually disintegrating into heaps of rubble. About 1910 Father John Raley came to Lompoc nearby and roused local interest in this work. In 1935, after lands had been given by the Catholic Church and by the oil company, Purísima Concepción became a California state park. Restoration work was taken over by the Civilian Conservation Corps. Before actual restoration was commenced, much time was spent in painstakingly gathering evidence through artists' on-the-spot sketches, excavation, and interviews with local old-timers to find out how the mission looked before secularization took place. Bricks of adobe were patiently made in the same manner as the originals had been, and where possible, the original adobes were used. Finally, on the day of the Pearl Harbor attack, Sunday, December 7, 1941, La Purísima Concepción was rededicated. It is really best described as a Mission-Museum for the restoration was to show how a Mission really looked in the height of Mission days. Today, it is most interesting because of its location, which is still quiet and rural, and because its setting and architecture closely resemble its 1820 appearance.

La Purísima Concepción is located 19 miles west of Buellton.

The Mission of Santa Cruz

Santa Cruz, the twelfth mission, was founded September 25, 1791. Today, nothing remains of the original buildings. Its early survival was a struggle. Some account for the decline of Santa Cruz by describing the proximity of the dissolute citizens of the civilian town of Branciforte, founded in 1797 on the opposite side of the Lorenzo River. Indeed, there were frequent difficulties between the neophytes and padres on one hand and the Branciforte citizens on the other.

The adobe church was erected in 1793 and 1794, but the mission was never successful, and frequent earthquakes helped destroy it. After the January, 1840 earthquake, a number of Santa Cruz's tiles were carried off. In 1851 the final disaster occurred when the walls of the church fell. Treasure seekers soon carried away the rest.

As early as 1835 secularization was more complete here than at any other mission. The region became a smuggling center for hides and tallow. Although Pio Pico placed the mission on the market in 1846, it was not sold, and between 1844 and 1853 it was only occasionally inhabited.

In 1931 Gladys Sullivan Doyle learned that the scattered vestments and other relics of Santa Cruz had been dispersed. Like her uncle, James D. Phelan, she had always been interested in California history, and she decided to have a replica of the mission built. It is about half the size of the original and contains some relics.

She was buried there, at the Baptistry, in 1933.

The replica is located at Emmet and School Streets in Santa Cruz.

The Mission of Nuestra Señora de La Soledad

The thirteenth mission seemed destined for misfortune almost from the very beginning. Father Juan Crespí is said to have christened the barren region "Soledad" which means solitude or aloneness. The origin of "Soledad" occurred when Father Serra was returning to Carmel from the founding of Mission San Antonio. In the area of Soledad he met some Indians and on asking a lady her name, she said something that sounded like the Spanish "Soledad." And Serra said "Here you have María de Soledad," (Our Lady of Solitude—a title given to the Blessed Virgin and applied to her on the days between Christ's death Good Friday and Easter Sunday.) Today one may only see the sadly crumbling adobe ruins and a large wooden cross marking the site.

Soledad was founded on October 9, 1791. Ten years later an epidemic was claiming several natives every week. Many converts ran away. Father Zephyrin Englehardt, noted California mission historian, has reported that two of its padres were downright hoodlums! These two, Mariani Rubí and Bartolomé Gili, were among the very few black sheep among Franciscan padres.

Soledad's years after secularization only prolonged the tale of tragedy. The mission roof fell in about 1874. J. Ross Browne, early California writer, observed that "A more desolate place than Soledad cannot well be imagined. The old church is partially in ruins, and the adobe huts built for the Indians roofless, and the walls tumbled about in shapeless piles. Not a tree or shrub is to be seen anywhere in the vicinity. The ground is bare, like an old road, save in front of the main building (formerly occupied by the priests), where the carcasses and bones of cattle are scattered about, presenting a disgusting spectacle."

George Wharton James in THE OLD FRANCISCAN MISSIONS OF CALIFORNIA, wrote: "In 1904 there was but one circular arch remaining in all the ruins; everything else had fallen in. The roof fell in thirty years ago. At the eastern end, where the arch is, there are three or four rotten beams still in place; and on the south side of the ruins, where one line of corridors ran, a few poles still remain. Heaps of ruined tiles lie here and there, just as they fell when the supporting poles rotted and gave way."

Recently, under the auspices of the Native Daugh'ers of the Golden West, restoration has been undertaken. The chapel was restored in 1954 and the padres' wing in 1963.

The restored mission is located on a side road off U.S. Highway 101, three miles southwest of Soledad.

Mission San José

The fourteenth mission was founded on June 11, 1797, some fifteen miles north of San Jose, California's first civilian pueblo. A new church completed in 1809, replaced the first wooden structure, but it was destroyed by the 1868 earthquake. Now only a portion of the old monastery remains, containing a few mementos of the mission. After the 1868 quake a new parish house and a new church were built nearby. The three bells of the old mission had survived secularization and were hung in the steeple of the new building. They still toll. The remains of the old adobe monastery were restored in 1916 and today form a museum.

As to the activities at Mission San José, even the search for a spot to build it was a daring undertaking in 1797, for the eastern shores of San Francisco Bay were not yet thoroughly explored. There were several great Indian uprisings in the area. An especially war-like chief, the Indian,

Estanislao, finally surrendered to General Mariano Vallejo. His name is perpetuated in the Stanislaus River and County where many of his offenses were committed.

Secularization occurred in 1836, and in May, 1846, Governor Pío Pico sold San José to his own brother, Andres Pico. The sale was ineffective. During gold rush days the mission region became a trading post. Sensationally large crops were grown there for the miners, but San José Mission had always been rich in agricultural produce. Raymund F. Wood tells us that its valleys were the most vertile of any in California except at Mission San Luis Rey.

In 1853 the name of the region was changed from "Mission San José" to "St. Joseph's Parish."

Mission San José is located on State Highway 21, 15 miles northeast of the city of San Jose.

San Juan Bautista, the fifteenth California mission, was founded on June 24, 1797. As they did in the case of nearly every mission, the Franciscan friars proved their genius for choosing an exceptional site in an area known to the Indians as Popeloutchom, and later known as San Benito. There were abundant trees for timber: willow, poplar, alder, and also tules for the roofing before tiles would be made. Only a mile away deposits of limestone and harder rock for the mission foundations could be obtained.

The present church, of adobe and brick, was built 1803-1812. It is cruciform as a result of the blocking of the side aisles. The interesting *reredos* in the church were decorated by Thomas Doak, first American resident of California. Doak had arrived from Boston about 1816. This building is the largest of all mission churches. It is also the widest and the only one with three naves. It is 160 feet long, paved with *ladrillos*, or large kiln-baked tiles.

In 1906 the great San Francisco earthquake forced the outer walls to cave in and part of the roof over them fell, but the filling in of the side aisles probably saved the church.

San Juan Bautista was quite an intellectual center. Father Estévan Tapis, who was buried there in 1825, was a famed musician, and his choir of Indian boys was known widely. Father de la Cuesta, who arrived at San Juan in 1808, staying 25 years, made the mission a scholarly place. He studied the Indian languages of that area and wrote a volume about them. But all was not peaceful study at the mission. The warlike Tulare Indians often threatened the area. The overthrow of Governor Manuel Micheltorena was plotted by Juan B. Alvarado and José Castro within the mission in 1839. San Juan became important during the gold rush, for stage horses were changed there. But in the 1870's a dread smallpox epidemic struck. Drought was added to this, and together they made the small community growing up about the mission a virtual ghost town.

In August, 1928 San Juan Bautista was put under the jurisdiction of the Maryknoll Fathers. Today it is administered by the Diocese of Monterey-Fresno. Buildings of historic interest surrounding the plaza of San Juan, including the hotel, became state property in September, 1935.

Today, visitors may see the interesting mission kitchen with its masonry ovens in especially good repair. Fine vestments of the padres are on view in the museum. In many ways, this is the best preserved of the missions. San Juan Mission with its plaza, Mission and surrounding buildings best of all exudes the atmosphere of the late Mexican period.

Located in the town of San Juan Bautista, this mission is located four miles south of U.S. Highway 101, 17 miles north of Salinas.

Nine miles north of Paso Robles stands mission number sixteen, San Miguel Arcángel. It was established on July 25, 1797, one of the four founded by Father Fermín de Lasuén that summer. San Miguel was prosperous from the start. The first day friendly Indians appeared with fifteen children to be baptized, and by 1815 the mission had 1066 converts.

The present church was built between 1816 and 1818 and decorated in 1821 by Estéban Munras from Monterey. It is the most poorly lighted of all mission church interiors, for there are only three windows. Yet the simple exterior hides a beautifully decorated interior. The great rafters and corbels were hewn from solid trees which faithful Indians brought forty miles from the mountains. The walls are designed to represent fluted pillars tinted blue, while between these are conventionalized designs of leaves and carved figures. The colors are still bright.

San Miguel never had a tower. Its bells hung on a wooden standard before the church or between corridor arches. The corridor arches are asymmetrical like those of some European churches.

Mrs. Fremont Older, who visited, cherished, and described all the missions, called San Miguel the "saddest mission," for here was committed one of the state's most frightful murders. By 1848 the mission had been secularized, its owner being William Reed. Reed told some former soldiers of the money he had made by selling some sheep. This was to be his last boast, for the ruffians to whom he had given hospitality soon returned and, in the room now used as a museum, killed Reed, his family and six servants. Then the five murderers fled with all the gold and valuables. However, three were killed by a posse and the others were executed at Santa Barbara, December 28, 1848. To this day some people insist that ghosts haunt San Miguel.

On September 2, 1859 the mission was destined for pleasanter times, for on that day President James Buchanan returned it to the Catholic Church. Since then, the once-roofless shops and padres' rooms have been restored. Each year the mission features the reenactment of the Posadas during the Christmas season. Since 1929 it has been under Franciscan administration. San Miguel is the novitiate of the Franciscans of the Santa Barbara province.

Mission San Miguel is located on old U.S. Highway 101, in the the town of San Miguel.

The Mission of San Fernando Rey de España

San Fernando was one of the two California missions dedicated to sainted kings. Ferdinand III, King of León and Castile, and cousin of St. Louis IX of France, was noted for his religious zeal and his victories over the Moors. He reigned during the first half of the thirteenth century and was canonized by Pope Clement X in 1671. He had been one of the greatest of Spanish kings. The mission named for him was founded on September 8, 1797, by Padre-Presidente Fermín de Lasuén, as the seventeenth mission.

Although San Fernando never attained the architectural beauty of several other missions, there are many interesting things to be seen. The long building, called "House of the Fathers," is the most prominent of the remaining structures; it has twenty-one rooms and was built between 1810 and 1823. Its reception room is the largest in the California missions. This building is 235 feet long by 65 feet wide, with an arched corridor, tiled roof, and unique bell arch. It contains a kitchen, guest room, chapel, quarters for the padres, refectory, a library, and offices of the mission. The unique little belfry at the west end is the only one on a mission building not connected directly with a chapel.

The church, built of adobe, was completed in 1806, but was badly damaged in the earthquake of 1812 and had to be rebuilt. After secularization of the missions, it fell into decay and has been but recently restored.

San Fernando had one of the best of mission smithies, which explains its most ornate grilles. Across the street from the mission, in Brand Park, are the remains of two reservoirs.

San Fernando was a center of history. The first gold and the first oil discovered in California were located near here.

After secularization the mission became a cattle ranch, but on May 31, 1862, President Abraham Lincoln signed a patent giving Mission San Fernando with 75 acres to the Roman Catholic Church. In 1896 Charles F. Lummis, as president of the Landmarks Club, raised money to restore the roof. In 1902 Father James E. Burns became the first permanent pastor since 1852. On August 4, 1916 San Fernando Candle Day was held. Six thousand people, regardless of creed, came forth, each bearing a flickering candle, the receipt for a dollar contributed to the restoration fund. The repaired church building was dedicated on Sunday, September 9, 1937.

On a visit, one will especially want to see the Moorish windows in the House of the Fathers, the holes cut in doors for the friars' cats to pass through, the copper brandy still, and murals in the guest room.

San Fernando Mission is located west of the city of San Fernando on Mission Drive, near Sepulveda Boulevard.

Most successful and most august of all the twenty-one missions was San Luis Rey de Francia. Named for St. Louis IX, King of France, it became, upon its founding, on June 13, 1798, the eighteenth Franciscan mission in Upper California.

Father Fermín Lasuén, *padre presidente* of all the missions after Serra's death, officiated at the founding, but Father Antonio Peyri soon took over at San Luis Rey. His farsighted work and eagerness for life, his genius as a builder, all helped make San Luis Rey the largest and one of the finest of missions. He remained in charge for 34 years, and when he left it is said that the Indians followed him to the shore and watched with tears as he sailed away. Later they placed flowers regularly before his portrait.

Many legends are told about his thirty-odd years of work in the area which he considered sacred. Associated with him was the scholarly Father Gerónimo Boscana, author of *Chinigchinich*, a book on his researches about the pagan god of the southern California Indians. In 1811 Peyri and Boscana planned the present magnificent church at San Luis Rey which was officially completed on October 4, 1815. The dome was not finished until 1829, and one tower was never built.

In every way, San Luis was successful. It is said to have had the lowest death rate of all California missions. By 1828 it produced annually 16,497 bushels of grain, while 58,765 animals were on its ranges and 2736 Indians worshipped and lived on its grounds. One can still see at the mission what is reputed to be the oldest and first pepper tree in California. This tree (*schinus molle*) was introduced to California from Peru about 1830 by some sailors and planted at the mission by Peyri.

At the time of secularization, San Luis Rey was valued at $300,000. The fathers there still show visitors Abraham Lincoln's signature on a document returning the mission in 1865 to the Catholic Church.

When Father Joseph O'Keefe arrived in 1893, the mission was falling into ruins. During his twenty years of service he supervised its reconstruction. Indeed, it had been ill-used before his coming, for a liquor shop had been kept there and later, the mission was sold.

San Luis Rey was rededicated on May 12, 1893. Although the tower crashed on July 22, 1926, it has been restored. One may still see one of the few remaining mission fountains before the church. Today, San Luis Rey is a house of study for future Franciscan missionaries. There they pursue their college course.

It is located in the town of San Luis Rey, five miles east of Oceanside, just off State Highway 76.

The Mission of Santa Inés

Saint Agnes, like Saint Barbara, was a Roman maiden who suffered martyrdom. She was an outstanding beauty sought by many nobles, but refused them all, saying that she was espoused to a heavenly bridegroom. Because she was a Christian in a pagan land, Agnes was condemned to death. She is the patron of young girls. Her mission was the last one founded south of the Golden Gate. It was founded on September 17, 1804 by Fray Estévan Tápis, the only mission established under Tápis' presidency. That day, a brush *enramada* was erected, and eventually an adobe church was constructed, only to fall during the earthquake of December 21, 1812. A new structure, begun in 1815, was dedicated on July 4, 1817. This church, of adobe faced with brick, still stands. The interesting *campanario* collapsed in 1910, was reconstructed poorly of concrete, but has been modified since.

In building Santa Inés, workers traveled 45 miles into the mountains to get pine, sycamore, and oak for the rafter timbers. Nails were scarce, so the beams and rafters were bound together with rawhide strips. Sea shells supplied lime. The walls were protected by a gluey preparation of prickly cactus soaked in water, which gave a smooth, whitewashed appearance. The walls of the church interior were decorated, between 1818 and 1820, with murals done by the Indians.

In 1824 a serious Indian revolt against the mistreatment of the neophytes by the soldiers broke out; harness shops and storerooms were burned. It is said that an Indian girl ran all the way from the Tulare region to warn of the impending attack and died from exhaustion at the mission she saved.

The first seminary in Alta California, The College-Seminary of Our Lady of Guadalupe, was established at Santa Inés in 1844 by California's first bishop, Francisco Garcia Diego y Moreno. By 1845, thirty-three students attended, but no women were admitted. There was also a primary school with tuition and board at $150, but its existence was precarious and enrollment pitifully small.

In 1850 the Franciscans left Santa Inés and decay set in. President Lincoln, as he had in the cases of several other missions, restored Santa Inés to the Church, in 1862. By 1881, however, the College had been abandoned. Three years later, half of the front colonnade was in ruins. One may still see the 19th pier standing alone.

At the turn of the century, an Alsatian, Father Alexander Buckler, made the first real effort to repair and restore the buildings. With the aid of homeless men he housed and fed, Father Buckler turned the shambles into a fair facsimile of what the mission once had been. Neighbors marveled at "Padre Alejandro's tramps" who brought order.

Today, there are plans to restore the whole mission compound as it once looked. Visitors are welcomed by Capuchin Franciscan fathers and may see some of the finest art treasures preserved at any mission.

Mission Santa Inés is located in the town of Solvang on State Highway 150, seven miles east of Buellton.

The Mission of San Rafael Arcángel

Sixteen miles north of San Francisco, California's twentieth mission, San Rafael Arcángel, was founded on December 14, 1817. Its founder, Vicente Sarría, was aided by Padres Abella, Gil, and Durán.

At first San Rafael was not a mission, but merely an asistencia, or sub-mission, attached to San Francisco. It was founded for an unusual reason—the health of the Indians of the Bay region. Here then was a mission that began as a health resort! It was believed that this area, inland from San Francisco's coastal fogs, would be salubrious.

In 1818 a simple church and mission houses were built, but now all have disappeared, to be replaced by a modern church. (A copy of the original mission church was constructed nearby about 1950.) Ruins set in early. Already in the 1860's, while gypsies camped in the orchards and vineyards, one could say, "Of all California missions, San Rafael Arcángel, has been the most completely obliterated."

San Rafael, or St. Raphael, was the patron saint said to heal body and soul. Appropriately enough, therefore, the asistencia-to-become-a-mission was named for him. During its brief existence San Rafael acquired no tower, no belfry, no gables. The bells were suspended from a heavy beam on a standard outside the church.

In 1823 San Rafael was elevated to the rank of a mission, independent of San Francisco de Asis. In spite of several Indian conflicts it prospered for a time and shipped supplies to the infant mission at Sonoma to the north. John Bidwell, the "Prince of California Pioneers," who had brought the first covered wagon train overland to California in 1841, said that San Rafael produced the best grapes of any mission. John C. Frémont and his soldiers, during the course of the Mexican War, took possession of the mission on June 26, 1846, but this was its last major role in the now fast-moving history of California.

This mission is located in the city of San Rafael about 16 miles north of San Francisco.

Northernmost of California's missions, the last to be established, and the only one founded while the province belonged to Mexico, was the Mission of San Francisco Solano. Its patron, St. Francis, Apostle of Peru and the Indies, died in South America in 1610.

Padre José Altimira, who founded the mission on July 4, 1823, was new to the Western Hemisphere. Born in Barcelona, Spain, young and optimistic, he had new ideas for mission founding. Seeing that Dolores Mission at San Francisco was failing because of poor soil and severe climate, he decided to establish a new mission in a beautiful valley which is today called "The Valley of the Moon" because, as the Indians had observed, when the moon rose farthest north in winter, it appeared seven times in succession as it swung behind seven distinct peaks before floating clear.

Altimira believed that many Indians in the region might be converted and eventually defend Mexican claims to the region against the encroaching Russians. Russian advances had already brought the Muscovites to Fort Ross not far away on the coast just north of the mouth of the Russian River.

The mission's founding was not at first sanctioned by the Padre-President of California missions, Vicente Sarría, but later he approved and the governor gave his consent. In 1826 a severe Indian attack barely allowed Altimira time to escape alive. Neophytes came in large numbers, 693 by the end of 1824. By 1832 the peak of 996 was reached, small for most missions. In 1834 the mission was secularized.

In 1835 Vallejo, one of California's wealthiest and best educated men, laid out the new town of Sonoma. It boasted California's largest plaza, covering eight acres. On June 14, 1846, 32 Americans, led by Ezekiel Merritt, fearing that Mexican authorities were about to oust all foreigners from California, revolted against Mexican rule, arrested Vallejo, and raised the Bear Flag of the California Republic.

In 1881 the arch-bishop of San Francisco sold the mission to Solomon Shocken for $3000. For another thirty years hay was stored in the mission church. The simple adobe walls were disintegrating when the California Landmarks League with Congressman Joseph R. Knowland as president, collected through William Randolph Hearst's San Francisco *Examiner* the sum of $13,000 with which to buy the mission, which was then given to the State of California.

The state restored the mission as it had looked when Lt. Colonel Victor Prudon saw and sketched it after the Mexican War. Finally, in October, 1922, the building was opened to the public as a museum as Sonoma Mission State Park. It is undistinguished as to architectural details, but fascinating because of its brief but colorful role in the history of Mexican California.

The Solano Mission is located in the town of Sonoma on State Highway 12 about forty-three miles north of San Francisco.